# Journey

*A 30-day Affirmation and Testimonial Journal Towards Your Journey 2 Peace*

- *Chapter 1:The Vision*
- *Chapter 2: I Can't Change History*
- *Chapter 3: The Residue of Abuse*
- *Chapter 4: The Vision*
- *Chapter 5: Never Feel Guilty*
- *Chapter 6: Bow Down*
- *Chapter 7: Set A Reminder*
- *Chapter 8: Don't Apologize For Love*
- *Chapter 9: Perception Vs. Reality*
- *Chapter 10: Don't Rush The Healing*
- *Chapter 11: Share Your Testimony*
- *Chapter 12: God Allowed It*
- *Chapter 13: It's Worth It*
- *Chapter 14: Be In A Relationship With Yourself*
- *Chapter 15: Manna*
- *Chapter 16: Family Is Deeper Than Blood*
- *Chapter 17: Its Not All About You, Boo*
- *Chapter 18: Don't Box Yourself In*
- *Chapter 19: Healing Hurts*
- *Chapter 20:Enjoy Life On Your Own Terms*
- *Chapter 21: The Spirit of Your Ancestors*

- *Chapter 22: Re-Invent Yourself*
- *Chapter 23: Love is Growth*
- *Chapter 24: Yaaassss!!!*
- *Chapter 25: Revolutionary Love*
- *Chapter 26: Choose your Battles*
- *Chapter 27: Don't Believe Me Just Watch*
- *Chapter 28: God Will Hold Your Position*
- *Chapter 29: Your Already Free.....Live it!*
- *Chapter 30: Leave Footprints*
- *Chapter 31: It Will Get Better*

**ISBN-13:978-1548070281**

**ISBN-10:1548070289**

*SquashBlossom Publishing*

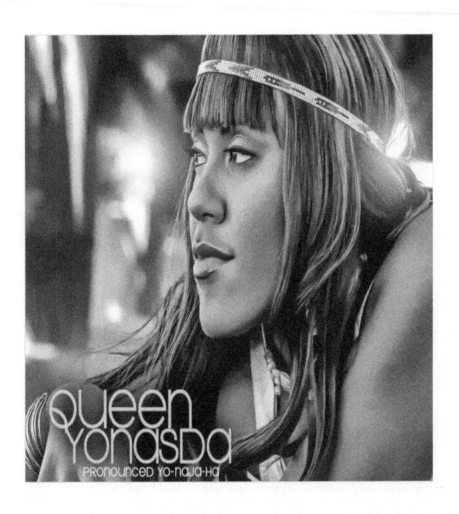

queen
yonasda
PRONOUNCED YO-NAJA-HA

# Chapter 1

# The Vision

In order for us to get on this journey to ultimate peace we must envision ourselves there. Many of us always seem to tell ourselves, "all I want is peace!" We say it but never make the concrete steps to fulfill it. We don't have to die to feel what heaven feels like. We either can make our daily lives a living hell or a heavenly heaven, its up to you!

I am writing this book, not because I am at ultimate peace, but I am in a place where my peace today is better than yesterday. I have learned from my mistakes, and maybe making new ones. But the beautiful part is I am willing to share my journey with you. This is not my autobiography. I have begun writing daily posts on my social media called **#Road2Peace**. I began sharing my journey to peace, because here I was in a marriage where I *"played"* joy, I *"showed"* happiness, and we made the *"image"* of love look great. But truthfully it was far from that. I was broken. I was very unhappy and also losing my smile, losing my laughter, losing my joy, and losing my peace. When he left, he left me and my son homeless. While we stayed with different friends and family, I began to get those *"Ah-ha"* moments of *"Oh there goes that laugh"* or *"Oh THATS why I remain to stay, cuz of my ego, putting all my hope and faith into him and not God, etc. etc."*

See when we go through pain we must find the joy, if not we will forever be in pain. I was determined to find my joy again, my love again, my peace again. It wasn't going to happen overnight, it was going to be a journey. A journey to peace. Welcome to YOUR *#Journey2Peace.*

Mitakoye Oyasin

All My Relations

YoNasDa LoneWolf

# GOD TAKE THE WHEEL

Wake up today feeling great! There is soooo much more you can do but I know without God's permission nothing is permissible! You and I can plan but HIS plans is always the right plan! So today lets put our hands up and say "God take the wheel!"

*So today as you plan your day just be ready when God takes the wheel and moves to the right, when you planned on going left! He's in control!!*

I can't change history but use my wisdom to make better decisions #roadtopeace

DAY 2

# I CAN'T CHANGE HISTORY

Live with no regrets of your choices but choose to make better ones. We can't continue to let the choices that we made in the past determine who we are today. These choices become experiences. These experiences become knowledge. The knowledge becomes understanding and today make your past choices become wisdom.

*So today stop looking back on your past mistakes and choose to live better today!*

# THE RESIDUE OF ABUSE

The residue of abuse is a semi permanent

stain, just when you think your cleaned from it , something happens that reminds you how damaged you really are. When off of one action you began crying, your heart drops and you have a fear that's unimaginable and you aren't anywhere near your abuser.... It's like that oil stain that can't be removed from silk.

*Today, ask God to help you cleanse you from the residue from all mental spiritual, physical, and emotional abuse. Began to write out the earliest point in your life where you felt abuse. Continue going back to that moment until you don't feel the emotional attachment to it. You can't let that stain remain on you. Surprisingly there is a way to get out that stain in fabric, and there is also a way to get that abuse stain off of you.*

## DAY 4

# NEVER FEEL GUILTY

There is nothing wrong with moving on from being treated wrong. Never feel guilty for recognizing your worth.

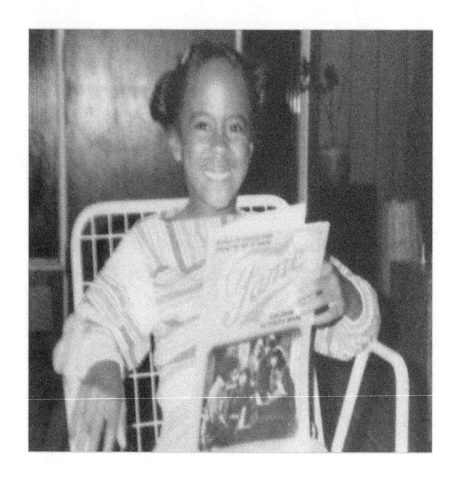

# BOW DOWN

Many would ask if I named myself "Queen
" and I told them " no" ever since I was a

little girl I was called Queen. Not princess but a queen I guess it's because I always walked like I owned the place or they saw something in me I didn't foresee. When I met Cappadonna he called me "Queen" and told me instead of just my name Yonasda I should be called "Queen YoNasDa" because maybe he fore saw something in me I didn't see.

From girls to women we don't actually see our own potential until someone brings it out of us. Our queen-ness is an evolving cipher to another cipher of empowerment. Yes there were times I yelled at some people, yeah there were times I put on my sneakers and marched against injustices, yes there were times I confronted people that disrespected my home and family. And yes there were times I was dressed in short skirts and heels and also covered from head to toe and spoke in front of thousands but NONE of that took me away from being a QUEEN!!! That's what makes us

QUEENZ!! We will fight for respect, freedom justice and equality and most importantly love but we won't disrespect ourselves in the     process and it's those around us that notice our queendom we just be who we are and let others give us the title!! So Queenz no matter how they come at you stand firm on your deen, on your square and let everyone else that can't respect you BOW DOWN!!!!

DAY 6

# SET A
# REMINDER

It's crazy. this homeless lady I met told me "this is the first time I actually have been able to have some quiet time to talk to God"

Don't let you being homeless, losing your job, on your death bed to FINALLY talk to God! Even when you are doing great , family is good, job is good, and your happy everyday, still talk to God! Praise HIM!!  At 3pm everyday I have an alarm that goes off on my phone that states "Praise God" which means that at 3pm everyday no matter what I'm doing, who I'm with, I shut out the world and just Praise HIM and thank God for everything.

It was a reminder to myself to NEVER put no one in front of my CREATOR!! That no matter what work I was doing, the kids I am balancing, the marriage I was trying to maintain, that none of this would be possible without God being first!!! On this journey I'm learning that I put God first but I didn't put me second and that's the part we ALL sometimes forget!

*Today put YOU second and today put God First!*

# DAY 8

# DON'T

# APOLOGIZE

# FOR LOVE

Don't never apologize for your love, cuz I'm sure I will never apologize for loving the way I loved!! I use to tell my past relationships "It's ok you don't love, my love!" They would look at me with shock. But think about it. When you truly love someone you may express it in your own particular, original way but its ok. If she or he cheated on you, don't try to blame yourself on "maybe if I gave him more attention" or "maybe I should have taken her on a vacation." Don't apologize for the way YOU love. That's how you love and its ok if that person didn't want to receive your love that way.

*So today stop apologizing for the way you love.*

# PERCEPTION V.S. Reality

Perception vs. Reality is a major cause of bad relationships with people. For instance many perceive a situation to be more of there liking but not of what it actually is. For example, you are going out with someone, communicate all the time, and within two days of not speaking you assume this person has a personal issue with you because you perceived them to be all about you but their reality maybe a death in the family or some personal things they had to do and just didn't have the time to reply back to you. So because you didn't know this "reality" you went off of perception and cursed them out, blocked them, etc etc and just like that you lost a close friend. See many of us do this, I have done this a couple of times assuming what I want their reality to be, "perception", instead of knowing the actual reality. But after growing up around many busy people and managing artists I learned that their intentions were pure and it's ok if they didn't come with how YOU wanted their reality to be in responding to you. That's why communication is key BEFORE judging that person! That's why quieting your spirit is important before getting emotional.

*So Today, stop assuming and get the facts, before you lose your friends, family and your mind.*

Day 10

# Don't rush the healing

A decade of what you felt was right and truth, the games that was being played, was all there to break all the good qualities of yourself, that the sacrifices you made was being taken for their own selfish gain, that the unconditional love you gave ,was really on their conditions.... So yes the healing is a process it will not happen over night. I'm learning to live my life the way I feel to live it without no rules and regulations! I'm re-learning happiness without anyone there so I can get back to loving myself first. Yes I'm not getting younger, yes I have two healthy boys and I want a daughter. But please don't rush the healing that I asked God to heal me from. Don't belittle my past or try to come up with YOUR story after the story was told. I'm now living life!! Don't judge that and don't box me into a false image on how YOU want me to heal.

*Today, heal on your own terms.*

Day 10

# Share Your Testimony

Just when you think you have leaped over the hurdle of pain then a certain song comes on that reminds you of the person that hurt you.

It's not an easy walk when you walk away from a relationship especially a marriage, especially when the other person treated you like you were their worst enemy. We "get busy" so we don't let experiences of laugh and tears cloud our mind. We post pictures of smiles to show them or their friends and family that "we moved on and happier without them" but it's not an instant Road To Peace it's a journey it's an awakening of self and decisions to "repeat or not repeat!" Since my #roadtopeace post I've received a lot of horrific stories of other people going through some things I hate to hear that they are going through.

Our testimonies is to let you know your not alone. Our testimonies is to let you know yes honey, I understand and maybe over stand why you got cheated on. Why your homeless with kids. Why you got abused.

Why people talked down to you, etc etc. our testimonies are to let you know I AM A Conquerer!!! I am a survivor!! I heard from a Minister that sometimes we are sooo use to just living through our pain that we haven't even realized we Conquered many obstacles!!! Yes baby you are a Conquerer !!! You came out that war a little bruised but you are still standing!!

*Today share your testimony, you maybe able to save a life.*

## Day 11

# God Allowed It

God only allowed it cuz HE
knew you can get through it!!!!

Day 12

# It's worth it

It's going be a long road but it's nothing that I haven't walked through before. I already went through the trenches with bombs, shots fired etc but I know I will be able to say that it was ALL worth it!!!!!

*Today, instead of getting depressed, stand up look in the mirror and say "Its ALL worth it!!"*

Day 13

# Be in a relationship with yourself

I've been in a relationship for a total of ten

years and married for four years within this time we separated for a month , then got back together and then six months off, then got back together and then a year ,then got married and then another year and then I file for a divorce and then reconcile and then we are back being separated and divorced. A crazy cycle, right?!

Sometimes in relationships we don't know why we continue to get drawn back into the same relationship because becoming ONE is a difficult task it's not easy especially as the two of you grow into different paths. I'm learning that no matter whom I'm in a relationship with I must find "oneness" with myself to find complete happiness with myself and loving myself. We front a lot in being happy with ourselves but when your in a relationship many of us including myself have put ALOT of pressure on our partner to "make" us happy and that's where we get it mixed up. Think about how selfish it is of you to put all that pressure on the person you love "to make YOU happy." That is alot of pressure on ONE person.

*So today and starting tomorrow began a relationship with your self first and with God and watch everything fall in perfect placement in your life*

Day 14

# Manna

When I was on the road on trying to get
stable, God was presenting to me people

that whether they were about to lose their home or were homeless and even though I'm not rich ,Gods favor and grace has gotten me by to be able to help others. I went into a gas station and this lady had two kids who left her abusive husband. She was asking people for food, not money but food. I told her I didn't have a lot but I will take her grocery shopping I spent $45 on food for her and her kids. She said that "God works in mysterious ways and that for me not to look at what I see but have faith that God will work everything out".

She said she got on a greyhound without her husband knowing where she is at and she met a manager at the local extended stay hotel who gave her a room for free for a month and hooked her up with a job at Jcpenny, which she gets paid Friday. Her children was happy when I gave them the groceries. We all go through tough times but someone can be going through it worse ,it's God's test on can we give when we feel we have nothing more to give?

In the bible it speaks about "manna". Manna looked like coriander seed and tasted like wafers made with honey (v. 31). When the Israelites saw it, they asked each other, "What is it?" (Heb. man hu [aWh'm]). This led to the name "manna, " "what?" It came each morning, except on the Sabbath day. It could be collected each day for that day alone, and only as much as could be eaten in one day. If a person tried to collect more than needed or to store the manna for future needs, it would grow wormy and foul (v. 20). In this way it was impossible for the Israelites to evade total dependence on God or to use the manna greedily for personal gain. Miraculously, the manna could be preserved on the sixth day and eaten on the Sabbath, and it was not to be found on the Sabbath morning (vv. 22-29). *So Today, take each day as a blessing and have enough faith that God will provide all your needs.*

Day 15

# Family is Deeper than Blood

I grew up during a time where a village

raised a child. None of these people lived in my neighborhoods, some of them lived across the country. The beauty of this village my mother had us in, is they were great friends of hers that assisted her on raising Julio and I. As I got older many people didn't understand why I called soo many people my cousins, aunties and uncles and would say comments like "blood is thicker than water " because they didn't understand how these people stepped into roles with unconditional love and loyalty and they didn't have to. When my mother passed, as alone as I felt I remember my mother telling me that she believes I'm going to be the one that will still stay in contact with the family "the village" and she said "make sure your there for them as they were their for us". So today I am grateful for the village that raised me. I could've been on the streets with my two kids right now but the same village that was always there is the same village that allowed me and my sons to stay with them until I'm back on solid ground again. They were there when my mother was running from the Feds and she needed a place to stay and they opened their home. They were the ones that spanked my behind if I needed it and hugged me when I needed

that also. I want to thank ALL of my mothers friends and family that never let go of me after she passed and still embraced me as a daughter and sister. Who you are is a pure reflection and the beauty of my mother and I thank you!!! There is too many to name to thank but you know who

you are. So today remember that "the blood " of Jesus was a symbol of the strength and obedience of God that he sacrificed for God's children and that blood is what makes us all related. Family isn't always about your blood line , family is about us doing and obeying the laws of God with each other, blood or not! Stop treating each other with selfishness and turning the other cheek on their kids problems or their issues. Help one another! Inspire them and their children. Take your single mother friends kids out and babysit so your friend can have some "Me Time!" Cook dinner for your married couple friends. Mentor children. Just remember even though you may leave this earth alone their is also a large amount of angels and relatives helping you get to the other side so you might as well start learning to live in God's village today because you are never alone.

*Today, began birthing your village.*

Day 16

# Its not all about you, boo!

When your going through just remember someone's going through something worse and I'm learning that my struggle isn't anyone's struggle but my own!

*Today, as you may run into trials tell yourself, "It ain't all about you, boo!"*

Day 17

# Don't box yourself in

Lately I've been around healers from all types. It's funny I told my cousin that I'm gonna turn into a chanting, yogi, incense in hand, post it note, gardening Christian muslimah indigenous hip hop b-girl. It's beautiful to know that if your a well rounded person you can related to people from all walks of life. Expand your knowledge of what you don't know. Listen and don't talk and watch what you learn. Go to a German festival, the Chinese festival learn outside of yourself because when you do this you'll learn the value of God's creation.

*Today get uncomfortable, and get out of your comfort zone.*

Day 18

# Healing Hurts

Healing from within hurts it's not all laughs. I told someone during my journey to peace that if I snap or am short with her, be patient with me because I'm healing. It's similar to someone putting on alcohol on a wound before putting the bandaid on, you say a quick. "Ouch", but the healing has begun.

I haven't seen my father since I was 13 and in 2015 I saw him. It was a beautiful time to get to know him as an adult daughter and an adult father perspective.

I now know why I ended up with men that were tall handsome from NYC but was never there. My father gave me a jewel I won't forget "I deserve a ReAL man A King!! No insecure, no selfish man a man that loves my sons and me," The healing began. My foundation of my life choices started with my parents and my family and I thank God for giving me the opportunity to began my healing process there.

*So Today its totally normal to still be hurt as you are in the process of healing. A cut doesn't turn into a scab over night. Its a process that you must be patient and nurturing to your wound in order for a complete healing. Don't allow anyone to tell you when you should be healed. Do allow an opening within your heart to heal.*

Day 19

## Enjoy life on your terms

I have realized the older I get the more I enjoy life... And if you enjoy it on your own terms ,nothing and no one can change that.

*Today, breathe in the air. Smile and dance to the music in your head and enjoy this wonderful experience called "life".*

Day 20

# The spirit of

# your ancestors

Just know you are the

fight of Crazy Horse the spiritual warrior of
Sitting Bull

The free spirits of Harriet Tubman

The knowledge of Angela Davis,
Malcolm X and the wisdom of Farrakhan

The answers to the prayers of Cinque,
Sojourner Truth and Shaka Zulu The gods
of Buddah, Jesus and Abraham You are
perfectly designed created by God And
with everyone that paved the way before

you You are the living truth that there is a
God that still loves us!!

*Today you are the answer to the prayers of
your ancestors.*

Day 21

# Re-invent yourself

Change is wonderful. When we are younger we are instructed to know what we wanna be when we get older. Some of us want to be a doctor, a nurse a singer, etc.

When I was younger I would tell people I wanted to be a singer, dancer. I danced on Soul Train, Teen Summit, Planet Groove and for various artists and saw it didn't pay a lot. When asked again at 18 what I wanted to be, I answered "the next female Russell Simmons a music mogul" until I worked at Polygram Records and countless indies and saw that artists should have the freedom to share openly and not from ceo's dictating what sells and what doesn't. So I began rhyming... Until my mother passed and then I was motivated to began using my testimony , my music , my culture and resources as a tool to bridge communities and speak across the country on cultural diversity. I then began writing in The Final Call and other publications. I restarted my music career, which got me even more in various communities still promoting freedom, justice and equality

and cultural diversity and unification. Who would ever thought that the young girl that wanted to be a singer would end up being an activist, rapper, writer, manager, and a

leader.If your in a place where you hate your job or career choice it's ok. Who said that you had to be a doctor, lawyer, retail manager forever? It's ok to do something out of your "resume skills". Step out on faith and move into your passion. The Hon. Min. Louis Farrakhan said that the ultimate joy is working and doing what God desires you to do: your passion. What are you passionate about ??? If you wasn't getting paid for it and you didn't care as long as you was doing your passion what would it be? Be 50 years of age or 20 years old it's never too late to jump and do what you desire to do. Stop living your life with this crazy way of thinking that just because you spent over $50k to be an engineer in school ,you graduated got a great paying job to be an engineer but you dread going to work everyday because you have a passion to be a chef. Be a chef !!! Nobody is going to live your life but you. Change is inevitable!!! It's ok! When you feel uncomfortable that's when God is moving in your life.

**Today began to re-invent yourself and get uncomfortable!**

Day 22

# Love is growth

It feels soooooooooo good to have someone really appreciate and understand you without explaining too much.

I'm learning that when you meet someone you don't always have to began looking at that person as an immediate husband or wife. Love isn't about having an end goal. It's about growth. It's about just learning one another and keeping it to yourself. Social media or your friends and family doesn't need to know that you just met someone or dating someone because that's when they began thinking they are about to plan your wedding. Because I've been down this path many times I'm just on some growing with someone right now, Working on growing together and building on that. Learn about having an understanding that doesn't have rules of how I want them to be or rules on how they want me to be. Just accept each other and understand that. Just when you think you understand love and relationships it's always someone that comes around and teaches you how to make it fit for the evolving you. Just find someone that fits you now and your growth

Day 23

# Yasssss!!!!

Whenever I get in my feelings when I'm working with our people I always say to myself "it's not all about you,boo boo!" it helps me to focus on the assignment and to get out of my emotions. See when we are in our emotions ALL the time when we are working that's where stress comes in, that's when the energy in your home is uneasy, that's when the relationships you are always drama! Focus on your assignment, the bigger picture and watch God work!

In order to have a revolutionary love you have to be on the front line .... You can't be hiding in the back while your partner is on the front line fighting for your love!! That's NOT revolution!!   and that sure ain't gangsta!!!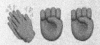

Day 24

# Revolutionary love

Day 25

# Choose your battles

Choose your battles wisely... Somethings

aren't worth it even if your right!! Bring peace in your life and give certain things to God. Once you give it to God just sit back, grab your popcorn and watch God fight the wrongs.

# Day 26

# Don't believe me just watch

Just tell those that keep on looking at your past to grab their popcorn and watch how God is transforming you into greatness!

Day 27

# God will hold your position

Through your transition, God will hold your position. Do not get upset as you see someone else get the promotion at your job. Don't get jealous of the family that got that house that you put in an application in for. Continue to be prayerful, grateful, humble, caring and loving and hard working and God will place you where He knows where you need to be and even in a greater place. Do not minimize what you want.

Day 28

# Your Already Free... Live it!

It's never too late to start over again. It's ok that job didn't work out. It's ok that your marriage or relationship didn't work out. It's ok that the new place or city you moved to isn't the ideal place to live.... It's all ok!!

Who said you have to stay there? Who said you must be miserable in a relationship that just doesn't do it for you? Who said the same way you packed your stuff up to live in that new city or new home you can't do it again. One thing some may hate or love about me is that I'm a free spirited person. In my younger years I may have been a little too all over the place.

If I'm at a restaurant and I ordered

something I thought I may like and it's not what I expected, best believe I will take it back and order something else. See that's how life should be. You should never put your life in situations where you are miserable and unhappy and accepting whatever trash comes with it. You only have ONE life!! Live it!! Stop expecting mediocrity and not greatness!! Live your life with God's rules and not man's rules!

And live a life with no regrets but with purpose and gain knowledge and wisdom from your choices!! Your already free.... Live it!!

Day 29

# Leave footprints

Make such a positive impact today that you leave footprints where others may follow.

Day 30

# It will get better

We ALL have "reasons" why we do this or don't do that!! Our history, our experiences aides our everyday decision making.

In the church there is a "testify" part of the program where people in the congregation come to the mic and tell the church "How God has been good to them!" And they would tell miracle stories, how God healed them, blessed them with certain material things they didn't see coming, sent Angels in the form of people to help them with depression, and many other things. I always loved this part of the service because it reminded myself that "my current dilemmas could've been worse" also that "God is still in the details of my life and that nothing was too BIG for God".

Our testimonies are a testament that there is a God! That HE can work it out.

2011 when I was pregnant I was on strict bed rest and in a deep depression because my husband left me 2 months after we found out I was pregnant so my brother moved in with me and helped me with my older son and also me. Everyday I struggled to see a tomorrow because I felt my tomorrow was getting worse and worse. Here I was 32 years old FINALLY married to a man I was with for 7 years and FINALLY having our baby and I couldn't be happy. I didn't want to be judged or be around people that would minimize my pain. I was in and out of the hospital because not only was my son growing inside of me I also was growing tumors at the same time ,which was very painful. I began going to church. I got very dedicated. I would come as I was, in sweatsuits, hair a mess sometimes. No one knew I am the granddaughter of the Minister or I am Wauneta LoneWolf daughter, or the wife of a known rap artist. I was able to go to the HOUSE of GOD and cry, scream, praise, worship God in a comfortable environment without the rules and judgment!

That became my healing place! It became my no flex zone!

I remember my former pastor told my brother that he ministers to the people to encourage them that they can make it through the week. Like myself and I know others, a week may feel like the end of the world! A week can feel like you won't be able to make it within the month. In this trial I was in, I lost many friends and some thought I was going crazy. But I'm here to tell you that there is A GOD!! That spoke to me when no one would speak to me. One thing Hon. Min. Louis Farrakhan always told me is to cling to God and once you do everything else will work out in your life.

To anyone reading this that are going through, You are NOT alone!! I know it feels like you are being judged, laughed at, alone, abandoned but what worked for me was cleansing myself with the word of God!! What helped me was going on sabbaticals, fast from social media, only talk to those that will fill you up with encouragement and not judgment. Don't wait on a "person" to save you because you'll be waiting ALONG time!! It's not the job of a woman or a man to come and fix your issues, they just as a mess as you are!! It's selfish of us to think these "people" are our Saviours when GOD is sufficient!! Don't worship idols!

The more you go through trials is to

strengthen your relationship with God and too much is given much is required and if your not going through a trial you need to asked yourself who you REALLY are clinging to, because the devil hates God's chosen!! So the devil will do everything in his power to have you disbelieve in God and that you will never get better. Best believe I've been there. So cling to God!! Stay focused on HIS promises in your life!!! And wash your self in HIS word!!! And eliminate false doctrine from satans helpers!

And as a living testament I'm here to tell you IT will get better!!!!

- Selah

Chapter 33

# Thank You's

This book is dedicated to all my close friends, family, people that I have met along my life journey thus far that played apart in sharing my testimony. My life works is dedicated to my two beautiful sons, my beloved mother Wauneta Lonewolf and my brother Julio.

-YoNasDa Lonewolf

@queenyonasda